W9-CRF-059

HOME-STYLE COOKING

Norma MacMillan

Picture credits

Paul Bussell: 13.
Alan Duns: 5, 21, 25, 33, 37, 45, 57.
Don Last: 61.
David Meldrum: 53.
Roger Phillips: 9, 17, 41, 49, 61.

Edited by Isabel Moore

Produced for K-Mart by

Marshall Cavendish Books Limited
58 Old Compton Street
London W1V 5PA

© Marshall Cavendish Limited 1981

First printing 1981

Printed in Singapore

ISBN 0 85685 943 5

CONTENTS

SOUPS

Philadelphia Pepper Pot

1 veal shank, sawn into 3 pieces
1 bouquet garni
6 peppercorns
6 quarts + 2 tablespoons water
1 lb blanched tripe, cut into 1 inch pieces
1 onion, chopped
2 large carrots, peeled and chopped
2 celery stalks, chopped
½ teaspoon red pepper flakes
2 medium potatoes, peeled and diced
2 tablespoons cornstarch
1 tablespoon butter

1. Put the veal shank, bouquet garni, and peppercorns in a Dutch oven and pour over the 6 quarts of water. Bring to a boil, skimming off any scum from the surface, then cover and simmer for 2½ hours.

2. Lift out the veal pieces and place them on a chopping board. Remove the meat from the bones and cut the meat into cubes.

3. Strain the stock and return it to the pan. Add the tripe, onion, carrots, celery, red pepper flakes, and salt and pepper to taste. Bring to a boil, cover and simmer for 1 hour.

4. Stir in the potatoes and veal cubes and simmer for a further 30 minutes or until the potatoes are tender.

5. Dissolve the cornstarch in the remaining water and add to the soup with the butter. Stir until thickened, then serve hot.

Serves 6–8

Yankee Bean Soup

$\frac{1}{4}$ *cup oil*
2 large onions, chopped
2 garlic cloves, crushed
6 tomatoes, skinned and chopped
4 celery stalks, chopped
1 cup dried red kidney beans, soaked overnight and drained
1 cup dried black beans, soaked overnight and drained
1 teaspoon sugar
1 tablespoon lemon juice
2 teaspoons dried thyme
2$\frac{1}{2}$ quarts beef stock

1. Heat the oil in a Dutch oven. Add the onions and garlic and fry until softened.

2. Add the remaining ingredients with salt and pepper to taste and stir well. Bring to a boil, then cover and simmer for 3 hours.

3. Taste and adjust the seasoning before serving.

Serves 6

Cajun Gumbo

½ lb cooked ham, in one piece
1 garlic clove, crushed
4 onions, chopped
¾ lb okra, sliced
1¼ lb raw shelled shrimp, deveined
1½ lb tomatoes, skinned and chopped
6 oz canned tomato paste
3 cups chicken stock
Tabasco sauce
1 green (bell) pepper, cored, seeded and chopped
1 lb cooked crabmeat, flaked
grated rind of 1 lemon
18 clams or mussels

1. Trim the fat from the ham and reserve. Cut the meat into cubes. Render the ham fat in a saucepan and pour off all but 2 tablespoons. Reserve the remaining fat.

2. Add the garlic, onions, and okra to the pan and fry for 10 minutes. Stir in the shrimp and cook for a further 5 minutes. Remove the shrimp and okra from the pan and set aside.

3. Add the tomatoes to the pan with the tomato paste, stock, and several dashes of Tabasco sauce. Bring to a boil and simmer for 1½ hours. Stir in the ham cubes and okra and continue simmering for 30 minutes.

4. Heat the reserved ham fat in a skillet. Add the green pepper and crabmeat and fry for 10 minutes, stirring frequently. Add to the tomato mixture in the saucepan, with the lemon rind, and shrimp. Stir well.

5. Place the clams or mussels on top of the gumbo. Cover the pan tightly and steam until they open. Serve hot.

Serves 6–8

Manhattan Clam Chowder

½ cup diced salt pork
1 onion, chopped
4 large tomatoes, skinned and chopped
3 medium potatoes, peeled and diced
½ teaspoon dried thyme
¾ cup tomato juice
2½ cups water
14 oz canned clams

1. Fry the salt pork in a saucepan until it has rendered its fat and the dice resemble croûtons. Remove from the pan and drain on paper towels.

2. Add the onion to the pan and fry in the pork fat until softened. Stir in the tomatoes, potatoes, thyme, and salt and pepper to taste.

3. Add the tomato juice, water, and juice from the canned clams. Bring to a boil, then cover and simmer for 12–15 minutes or until the potatoes are tender.

4. Stir in the clams and salt pork dice. Simmer for a further 5 minutes and serve hot.

Serves 6

(Top) Manhattan Clam Chowder
(Bottom) Pennsylvania Dutch Chicken Corn Soup

Pennsylvania Dutch Chicken Corn Soup

3 tablespoons oil
2 onions, sliced
4 celery stalks, chopped
2 quarts chicken stock
10 peppercorns
¼ lb egg noodles
2 cups chopped cooked chicken meat
1 lb canned corn kernels, drained
½ teaspoon dried sage
¼ teaspoon saffron powder

1. Heat the oil in a saucepan. Add the onions and fry until softened. Stir in the celery and fry for a further 3 minutes.

2. Add the stock and peppercorns. Bring to a boil and simmer for 20 minutes.

3. Stir in the remaining ingredients with salt and pepper to taste. Simmer for a further 15–20 minutes or until the noodles are tender. Serve hot.

Serves 4–6

SEAFOOD

Baked Shad with Cornbread Stuffing

2 shad fillets (about 1 lb)
6 tablespoons butter
2 tablespoons finely chopped scallions
2 tablespoons chopped green (bell) pepper
2 cups finely chopped mushrooms
¾ cup crumbled cornbread
¾ cup crumbled saltine crackers
1 teaspoon dried dill
½ cup water

1. Preheat the oven to 375°. Lay the fish fillets in a lightly greased shallow baking dish.

2. Melt 4 tablespoons of the butter in a skillet. Add the scallions, green pepper, and mushrooms and fry for 5 minutes. Stir in the cornbread and crackers with the dill, and salt and pepper to taste.

3. Spread the cornbread mixture over the fish fillets, then fold them lengthwise and tie in three places. Dot with the remaining butter and sprinkle with salt and pepper.

4. Pour the water into the baking dish and cover loosely with foil. Bake for 30 minutes.

5. Remove the strings, cut the fillets in half and serve hot, garnished with lemon wedges.

Serves 4

Shrimp Creole

2 tablespoons olive oil
2 large onions, finely chopped
1 garlic clove, crushed
1 cup dry white wine
1 lb canned tomatoes, drained and chopped
1 tablespoon red wine vinegar
1 tablespoon sugar
1 large green (bell) pepper, cored, seeded and chopped
1 large sweet red pepper, cored, seeded and chopped
1 tablespoon cornstarch
¼ cup water
1½ lb shelled shrimp, deveined

1. Heat the oil in a large skillet. Add the onions and garlic and fry until they are softened. Stir in the wine. Bring to a boil and simmer for 10 minutes.

2. Add the tomatoes, vinegar, sugar, and salt to taste and mix well. Continue simmering for 10 minutes.

3. Stir in the peppers and simmer for a further 10 minutes.

4. Dissolve the cornstarch in the water and add to the pan. Simmer, stirring, until thickened.

5. Stir in the shrimp and simmer for a final 5 minutes. Serve hot.

Serves 4

Shrimp Newburg

2 tablespoons butter
½ lb shelled shrimp, deveined
¼ cup Madeira or sherry
2 egg yolks
2 cups cream
cayenne pepper
hot cooked rice or buttered toast
chopped chives or parsley to garnish

1. Melt the butter in a saucepan. Add the shrimp and cook gently for 5 minutes.

2. Stir in the Madeira or sherry and cook for a further 2 minutes.

3. Lightly beat the egg yolks with the cream. Add to the pan with salt and cayenne pepper to taste and cook gently, stirring, until the mixture is thickened and creamy.

4. Pour over hot cooked rice or buttered toast and sprinkle with chives or parsley.

Serves 2

Crab Louis

1 cup mayonnaise
¼ cup heavy cream
¼ cup chili sauce
¼ cup chopped green (bell) pepper
2 tablespoons finely chopped chives or scallions
2 tablespoons chopped pitted green olives
lemon juice
1 large head of lettuce, shredded
3 cups flaked cooked crabmeat

1. Mix together the mayonnaise, cream, chili sauce, green pepper, chives or scallions, and olives. Add salt and lemon juice to taste. Chill this dressing.

2. Arrange beds of shredded lettuce on four serving plates and pile the crabmeat on top. Chill.

3. Top the crabmeat with the dressing and serve.

Serves 4

Jambalaya

3 bacon slices
1 onion, chopped
2 celery stalks, chopped
2 cups rice
2¼ cups chicken stock
¼ teaspoon cayenne pepper
1 bay leaf
1 large green (bell) pepper, cored, seeded and chopped
1 lb canned tomatoes, chopped with their juice
½ cup chopped cooked ham
1 cup chopped cooked chicken meat
½ lb shelled shrimp, deveined
chopped parsley to garnish

1. Fry the bacon in a saucepan until it is crisp and has rendered its fat. Remove the bacon from the pan and drain on paper towels. Crumble the bacon and reserve.

2. Add the onion to the pan and fry in the fat until softened. Stir in the celery and rice and cook, stirring, for 3 minutes. Add the stock, cayenne pepper, bay leaf, and salt and pepper to taste. Bring to a boil, then cover and simmer for 10 minutes.

3. Stir in the green pepper and tomatoes. Cover again and continue simmering for 5 minutes.

4. Add the ham, chicken, shrimp, and crumbled bacon and stir well. Simmer, covered, for a further 5 minutes or until the rice is tender.

5. Discard the bay leaf. Serve hot, sprinkled with parsley.

Serves 4–6

MEAT

London Broil

---

4 × ½ lb London Broil steaks
Marinade
¼ cup white wine vinegar
¼ cup oil
1 garlic clove, crushed
1 tablespoon lemon juice
4 peppercorns, coarsely crushed
1 teaspoon salt

1. Mix together the marinade ingredients in a shallow dish. Add the steaks and turn to coat with the marinade. Marinate for 2 hours at room temperature, turning the steaks occasionally.

2. Preheat the broiler. Drain the steaks and place them on the broiler rack. Broil for 6 to 8 minutes on each side, depending on how well done you like your steaks. Serve hot.

Serves 4

Meat Loaf

1½ lb ground round
¾ lb ground veal
¾ lb ground pork
4 slices of white bread
1⅓ cups milk
3 eggs
3 tablespoons finely chopped celery
2 onions, finely chopped
2 tablespoons chopped parsley
¼ teaspoon dried thyme
¼ teaspoon dried marjoram
¼ teaspoon dried basil
3 bacon slices
½ cup boiling water
¼ cup dry vermouth

1. Preheat the oven to 375°. Put all the meat in a large mixing bowl. Tear the bread into small pieces and soak in the milk.

2. Add the eggs to the meat with the celery, onions, parsley, dried herbs, pepper to taste, and bread and milk mixture. Combine the ingredients thoroughly, using your fingers.

3. Shape the mixture into a loaf and place it in a buttered loaf pan. Lay the bacon slices on top. Bake for 45 minutes or until the surface begins to brown.

4. Pour the boiling water over the meat loaf and continue baking for 45 minutes, basting once or twice with the vermouth and any juices that rise in the pan.

5. Unmold the loaf onto a warmed serving platter and serve hot.

Serves 4–6 with leftovers

Hamburger

3 lb ground round
1 cup fresh breadcrumbs
1 teaspoon dried thyme
1 egg, beaten
6 large hamburger buns, split

1. Preheat the broiler. Mix together the beef, breadcrumbs, thyme, salt and pepper to taste, and the egg, using your fingers to combine the ingredients thoroughly.

2. Divide the mixture into six portions and shape into burgers.

3. Arrange the hamburgers on the broiler rack and cook for 5 to 10 minutes on each side, depending on how well done you like your hamburgers.

4. Slide a hamburger into each bun and serve with sliced tomatoes, lettuce leaves, onion rings, catsup and relishes.

Serves 6

New England Boiled Dinner

1 × 4 lb corned beef brisket
1 onion, peeled
1 bouquet garni
1 tablespoon brown sugar
8 carrots, peeled
8 medium potatoes, peeled and quartered
6 small (pearl) onions, peeled
1 small head of cabbage, cored and cut into wedges

1. Place the beef in a Dutch oven and cover with cold water. Bring to a boil, skimming off any scum that rises to the surface. When the scum stops rising, add the onion, bouquet garni, and sugar. Half-cover and simmer for 2 hours.

2. Discard the onion and bouquet garni. Add the carrots, potatoes, and small onions. Continue simmering for 30 minutes. Add the cabbage wedges and simmer for a further 15 minutes or until all the vegetables and the meat are cooked through.

3. Remove the beef from the pan and carve it into slices. Arrange on a platter and surround with the drained vegetables.

Serves 6–8

Red flannel hash : Leftover New England boiled dinner can be made into this classic. Mix together 1 lb of cooked corned beef, 4 cubed cooked potatoes, $\frac{1}{2}$ lb cubed cooked beets and a chopped onion. Stir in $\frac{3}{4}$ cup of heavy cream, parsley, a teaspoon of Worcestershire sauce, cayenne pepper to taste. Melt butter in a large skillet, add the mixture and spread out evenly in the pan. Cook gently for 10 minutes, pressing down occasionally until a crust has formed on the base. Turn over and cook for 10 minutes or until a crust has formed. Serves 4.

Yankee Pot Roast

1 × 6 lb beef bottom round roast
2½ cups red wine
1 onion, thinly sliced into rings
4 garlic cloves, peeled
1½ teaspoons dried basil
2 tablespoons butter
1 lb canned tomatoes, drained
½ cup pitted black olives
1 tablespoon cornstarch
2 tablespoons water

1. Put the roast in a plastic bag. Add the wine, onion, garlic, and basil. Close the bag and marinate in the refrigerator for 6 hours, turning the bag over occasionally.

2. Preheat the oven to 350°. Remove the roast from the bag, reserving the marinade. Pat the roast dry with paper towels.

3. Melt the butter in a flameproof casserole. Put in the roast and brown on all sides. Pour in the reserved marinade and bring to a boil. Add salt and pepper to taste. Cover and place in the oven. Cook for 2 hours.

4. Add the tomatoes and continue cooking, covered, for 1 hour or until the meat is tender. Remove the roast from the casserole and carve it into thick slices. Arrange on a warmed serving platter and keep hot.

5. Strain the cooking liquid into a saucepan. Add the olives and bring to a boil.

6. Dissolve the cornstarch in the water and add to the pan. Simmer, stirring, until thickened. Pour the gravy over the meat and garnish with parsley.

Serves 10

Broiled Pork Chops

1 large onion, thinly sliced into rings
6 thick pork chops
Sauce
¼ cup red wine vinegar
½ cup tomato catsup
2 teaspoons sugar
½ teaspoon ground cloves
1 teaspoon celery seed
½ teaspoon mustard powder
1 bay leaf

1. Preheat the oven to 350°. Spread the onion rings over the bottom of a greased shallow baking dish that is large enough to hold the chops in one layer. Rub the chops with salt and pepper and place them in the dish.

2. Mix together all the ingredients for the sauce and pour over the chops.

3. Bake for 1 hour or until the chops are cooked through and tender. Discard the bay leaf before serving.

Serves 6

Baked Spareribs

2 tablespoons bacon fat or butter
1 onion, chopped
2 tablespoons vinegar
2 tablespoons sugar
¼ cup lemon juice
1 cup tomato catsup
3 tablespoons Worcestershire sauce
2 teaspoons sharp mustard
½ cup water
1 teaspoon dried basil
1 tablespoon chili powder (optional)
2 tablespoons chopped parsley
4 lb country spareribs

1. Preheat the oven to 450°. Melt the bacon fat or butter in a saucepan. Add the onion and fry until softened. Stir in the vinegar, sugar, lemon juice, catsup, Worcestershire sauce, mustard, water, basil, chili powder, if used, and parsley. Bring to a boil and simmer for 30 minutes.

2. Meanwhile, sprinkle the ribs with salt and pepper and arrange them on a rack in a roasting pan. Bake for 30 minutes. Drain the fat from the roasting pan. Remove the rack and place the ribs in the pan. Brush them with the cooked sauce.

3. Reduce the oven temperature to 300° and bake the ribs for a further 1½ hours brushing them frequently with the sauce.

Serves 4

CHICKEN

Creamed Chicken Livers

4 tablespoons butter
2 onions, thinly sliced into rings
12 chicken livers, cut into strips
1 cup cream
2 hard-cooked eggs, chopped
2 teaspoons paprika
hot cooked rice

1. Melt half the butter in a skillet. Add the onions and fry until golden brown. Remove the onions from the pan using a slotted spoon.

2. Add the chicken livers to the pan and fry for 5 minutes, stirring frequently. Remove the livers from the pan with a slotted spoon.

3. Add the remaining butter to the pan and melt it. Stir in the cream, eggs, paprika, and salt and pepper to taste. Return the livers and onions to the pan and mix into the sauce. Cook gently for 5 minutes.

4. Serve hot, with rice.

Serves 4

Chicken Maryland

3 tablespoons flour
1 tablespoon grated lemon rind
2 × 2 lb chickens, halved
2 eggs, beaten
1½ cups fresh breadcrumbs
oil for deep frying
4 tablespoons butter
4 bananas, peeled and sliced lengthwise
Corn fritters
1 cup flour
1 egg
¾ cup milk
1 cup corn kernels

1. Put the flour, lemon rind, and salt and pepper into a plastic bag. Add the chicken pieces and shake to coat them on all sides. Dip the chicken pieces in the beaten eggs, then coat with breadcrumbs. Repeat the egg-and-crumbing process, then chill the chicken for 2 hours.

2. Meanwhile, for the corn fritters, sift the flour and a little salt into a mixing bowl. Add the egg and milk and beat to make a smooth batter. Stir in the corn.

3. Heat oil in a deep fat fryer to 350°. Deep fry the chicken pieces, two at a time, for 15–20 minutes. Drain on paper towels.

4. Increase the heat of the oil to 375°. Drop heaped tablespoons of the corn batter into the oil and fry for 3 minutes or until puffed up and golden. Drain on paper towels and keep hot.

5. Melt the butter in a skillet. Add the bananas and fry for about 3 minutes or until golden brown on both sides. Serve the chicken with the fritters and fried bananas.

Serves 4

Chicken Tetrazzini

6 oz vermicelli
5 tablespoons butter
2 tablespoons flour
2 cups chicken stock
grated nutmeg
1 cup heavy cream
3 tablespoons pale dry sherry or white wine
3 cups shredded cooked chicken meat
½ lb mushrooms, sliced
½ cup fresh grated Parmesan cheese

1. Preheat the broiler. Cook the vermicelli in boiling water until it is tender. Drain and set aside.

2. Meanwhile, melt 3 tablespoons of the butter in a saucepan. Stir in the flour and cook for 3 minutes. Gradually stir in the stock. Bring to a boil, stirring, and simmer until thickened and smooth. Season with salt, pepper, and nutmeg. Stir in the cream, sherry or wine and chicken. Remove from the heat and keep hot.

3. Melt the remaining butter in a skillet. Add the mushrooms and fry briskly until just tender.

4. Spread the vermicelli out in a buttered flameproof dish. Scatter over the mushrooms. Pour the chicken mixture over the top.

5. Sprinkle with the cheese and broil just long enough to brown the top. Serve bubbling hot.

Serves 4

Chicken à la King

2 tablespoons butter
1 green (bell) pepper, cored, seeded and finely chopped
$1\frac{1}{2}$ cups thinly sliced mushrooms
1 tablespoon flour
1 teaspoon salt
$1\frac{1}{2}$ cups milk
1 cup cream
3 cups diced cooked chicken meat
3 egg yolks
2 teaspoons lemon juice
1 tablespoon paprika
2 teaspoons chopped parsley
3 tablespoons cream sherry

1. Melt the butter in a saucepan. Add the green pepper and fry for 5 minutes. Add the mushrooms and continue frying for 3 minutes.

2. Stir in the flour and salt and cook for 2 minutes. Gradually stir in the milk and cream. Bring to a boil, stirring. Add the chicken and mix well. Cook very gently for 5 minutes.

3. Lightly beat the egg yolks with the lemon juice, paprika, parsley, and sherry. Add about $\frac{1}{4}$ cup of the hot sauce from the pan, then stir this mixture into the remaining sauce. Continue cooking very gently for about 4 minutes. Do not let the mixture boil. Serve hot, with rice.

Serves 4

Brunswick Stew

5 tablespoons butter
8 chicken pieces
1 large onion, sliced
1 green (bell) pepper, cored, seeded and chopped
1¼ cups chicken stock
1 lb canned tomatoes, drained
½ teaspoon cayenne pepper
1 tablespoon Worcestershire sauce
½ teaspoon salt
1 cup canned corn kernels
2 cups canned lima beans
1 tablespoon flour

1. Melt 4 tablespoons of the butter in a Dutch oven. Add the chicken pieces and brown on all sides. Remove the chicken from the pan.

2. Add the onion and green pepper to the pan and fry until the onion is softened. Stir in the stock, tomatoes, cayenne pepper, Worcestershire sauce, and salt and bring to a boil. Return the chicken pieces to the pan. Cover and simmer for 40 minutes.

3. Stir in the corn and lima beans and continue simmering, covered, for 15 minutes.

4. Mix the remaining butter with the flour to make a paste. Add to the stew in small pieces and stir until thickened. Taste and adjust the seasoning before serving.

Serves 4–6

VEGETABLES & SALADS

Succotash

4 bacon slices
1½ cups canned corn kernels
1½ cups canned lima beans
6 tablespoons cream

1. Fry the bacon in a saucepan until it has rendered its fat and is crisp. Drain on paper towels. Crumble and reserve.

2. Pour off all but about 1½ tablespoons of the bacon fat from the pan. Add the corn and lima beans and heat through gently, stirring.

3. Stir in the cream, crumbled bacon, and salt and pepper to taste. Cook gently for a further 3 minutes or until piping hot.

Serves 4

Harvard Beets

1 lb beets
¼ cup sugar
1 teaspoon cornstarch
¼ cup vinegar
½ cup water

1. Put the beets into a saucepan and cover with water. Bring to a boil, cover and simmer for 50 minutes to 1¼ hours, depending on the size of the beets. Drain and, when cool enough to handle, peel and slice.

2. Mix together the sugar and cornstarch. Put the vinegar and water in a saucepan and heat until lukewarm. Stir in the sugar mixture and bring to a boil, stirring. Simmer for 2 minutes or until smooth and thick.

3. Add the beets to the pan and baste well with the sauce. Cook gently for 5 minutes or until the beets are heated through. Serve hot.

Serves 4

Boston Baked Beans

5 cups dried navy beans
2 teaspoons salt
1 large onion, chopped
½ lb salt pork, thickly sliced
¼ cup brown sugar
6 tablespoons molasses
1 tablespoon mustard powder
1 teaspoon pepper

1. Put the beans in a saucepan and cover with cold water. Add half the salt. Bring to a boil, then half-cover the pan and simmer for 30 minutes.

2. Preheat the oven to 250°. Drain the beans. Put the onion on the bottom of a casserole. Add a layer of beans, then cover with half the salt pork slices. Add the remaining beans and salt pork.

3. Mix together the sugar, molasses, mustard, pepper, and remaining salt. Pour into the casserole and add enough boiling water to cover the mixture.

4. Cover and bake for 5 hours, adding more boiling water from time to time so that the beans are kept covered.

5. Take off the lid and continue baking for 45 minutes or until a crust has formed on top. Serve hot.

Serves 6–8

Chef's Salad

1 head of lettuce, shredded
¼ lb cooked chicken meat, cut into strips
¼ lb cooked ham, cut into strips
¼ lb Swiss cheese, cut into strips
2 hard-cooked eggs, thinly sliced
1 tablespoon finely chopped onion

1. Put the lettuce into a large salad bowl. Arrange the chicken, ham, cheese, and eggs on top and scatter over the onion.

2. Serve with your favorite dressing, such as French, Thousand Island or Blue Cheese.

Serves 4

Caesar Salad

$\frac{3}{4}$ cup olive oil
4 slices of white bread, crusts removed and cut into small cubes
1 garlic clove, halved
2 tablespoons wine vinegar
1 teaspoon lemon juice
$\frac{1}{2}$ teaspoon Worcestershire sauce
$\frac{1}{4}$ teaspoon mustard powder
$\frac{1}{4}$ teaspoon sugar
2 heads of romaine lettuce, torn into pieces
1 egg
6 anchovy fillets, chopped
$\frac{1}{2}$ cup freshly grated Parmesan cheese

1. Heat $\frac{1}{4}$ cup of the oil in a skillet. Add the bread cubes and fry until golden brown on all sides. Drain these croûtons on paper towels.

2. Rub the cut surfaces of the garlic clove over the bottom and sides of a salad bowl. Discard the garlic.

3. Put the vinegar, lemon juice, Worcestershire sauce, mustard, sugar, the remaining oil, and salt and pepper to taste into the bowl. Mix well together.

4. Put the egg into a saucepan of boiling water and cook for 1 minute.

5. Meanwhile, add the lettuce to the salad bowl and toss to coat with the dressing. Scatter the anchovies, cheese and croûtons over the lettuce.

6. Break the egg on top. Toss the salad and serve immediately.

Serves 8

Blue Cheese Dressing

$\frac{1}{2}$ cup crumbled blue cheese
$\frac{1}{2}$ cup mayonnaise
$\frac{1}{2}$ cup heavy or sour cream

1. Beat the cheese into the mayonnaise, then beat in the cream.

2. Season to taste with salt and pepper and serve. Keep any leftover dressing in the refrigerator.

Makes $1\frac{1}{4}$ cups

Green Goddess Dressing

1 cup mayonnaise
2 anchovy fillets, finely chopped
3 scallions, finely chopped
2 tablespoons chopped parsley
2 teaspoons chopped fresh tarragon or 1 teaspoon dried tarragon
1 tablespoon tarragon vinegar
$\frac{3}{4}$ cup sour cream

1. Mix together the mayonnaise, anchovies, scallions, parsley, tarragon, vinegar, and pepper to taste.

2. Fold in the sour cream and chill for 30 minutes before serving. Keep any leftover dressing in the refrigerator.

Makes $1\frac{1}{2}$ cups

Mayonnaise, the basic ingredient in both Blue Cheese Dressing and Green Goddess Dressing.

DESSERTS

Maple Walnut Ice-Cream

1 cup maple syrup
3 eggs, separated
¼ teaspoon salt
1 teaspoon vanilla extract
1 cup heavy cream
½ cup chopped walnuts

1. Put the maple syrup in the top of a double boiler. Heat but do not let it boil.

2. Stir 2 tablespoons of the warm syrup into the egg yolks, then add this mixture to the remaining syrup in the pan. Cook gently, stirring, until the mixture thickens.

3. Stir in the salt and vanilla and remove from the heat. Cool, then chill for 1 hour.

4. Whip the cream until thick and fold into the maple syrup mixture. Beat the egg whites until stiff and fold in.

5. Remove the dividers from an ice cube tray and pour in the maple syrup mixture. Freeze for about 1 hour or until the mixture is frozen around the edges.

6. Tip the partially frozen mixture into a bowl and beat well. Stir in the nuts. Return the mixture to the ice cube tray and freeze for a further 3 hours.

Serves 4

Knickerbocker Glory

½ lb strawberries, hulled and halved
4 scoops of vanilla ice cream
4 ripe peaches, peeled, pitted, and sliced
4 scoops of chocolate ice cream
2 oz dark sweet chocolate
3 tablespoons brandy
¾ cup whipping cream
4 maraschino cherries

1. Divide the strawberries between four sundae glasses. Top each with a scoop of vanilla ice cream.

2. Divide the peach slices between the glasses and top with a scoop of chocolate ice cream.

3. Melt the chocolate gently with the brandy. Pour this sauce over the chocolate ice cream.

4. Whip the cream until thick and pipe or spoon it over the chocolate sauce.

5. Top each sundae with a cherry and serve.

Serves 4

Cherries Jubilee

1 lb canned Bing cherries, pitted
¼ teaspoon ground cinnamon
1 tablespoon sugar
2 teaspoons arrowroot
¼ cup brandy
vanilla ice cream

1. Drain the cherries, reserving 1 cup of the syrup.

2. Put the syrup in a saucepan and add the cinnamon, sugar, and arrowroot. Bring to a boil, stirring, and simmer until smooth and thickened.

3. Add the cherries and simmer for a further 2 to 3 minutes to heat them through.

4. Warm the brandy and add to the cherry mixture. Pour over vanilla ice cream and set alight. Serve flaming.

Serves 6

Strawberry Shortbread Cake

2 cups flour
½ cup confectioners' sugar
12 tablespoons (1½ sticks) butter
1 egg yolk
1½ cups whipping cream
1 lb strawberries, hulled
2 tablespoons granulated sugar

1. Sift the flour and confectioners' sugar into a mixing bowl. Add the butter and cut into small pieces. Knead to make a smooth dough, adding the egg yolk and 2 or more tablespoons of the cream. Chill for 30 minutes.

2. Preheat the oven to 375°. Divide the dough in half and roll out each piece to a 9 inch round. Place the rounds on well-greased baking sheets. Mark one of the rounds into eight wedges. Bake for 12–15 minutes or until the edges of the shortbreads are golden brown. Cool.

3. Slice the strawberries. Whip the remaining cream until thick and fold in the strawberries.

4. Place the unmarked shortbread round on a serving plate and pile the strawberry and cream mixture on top.

5. Break the second shortbread round into the marked wedges and arrange these over the cream filling. Sprinkle over the granulated sugar and serve.

Serves 8

Shoofly Pie

pie pastry made with $1\frac{1}{2}$ cups flour
$1\frac{1}{2}$ cups flour
8 tablespoons (1 stick) butter
1 cup brown sugar
1 teaspoon baking soda
1 cup boiling water
$\frac{1}{2}$ cup molasses
$\frac{1}{2}$ cup clear honey

1. Preheat the oven to 375°. Roll out the dough and use to line a 9 inch pie pan.

2. Sift the flour into a mixing bowl. Rub in the butter until the mixture resembles breadcrumbs. Stir in the sugar.

3. Dissolve the baking soda in the water, then stir in the molasses and honey. Pour the mixture into the pie shell. Sprinkle the flour and butter mixture over the top.

4. Bake for 10 minutes, then reduce the oven temperature to 350°. Continue baking for 25–30 minutes. Cool before serving.

Serves 4–6

Pecan Pie

pie pastry made with 1½ cups of flour
½ cup pecans
3 eggs
1 cup light corn syrup
½ cup brown sugar
½ teaspoon vanilla extract
¼ teaspoon salt

1. Preheat the oven to 425°. Roll out the dough and use to line a 9 inch pie pan. Bake unfilled for 20 minutes or until golden brown and set. Remove from the oven and cool slightly.

2. Arrange the pecans on the bottom of the pie shell in concentric circles.

3. Beat the eggs with the syrup, sugar, vanilla, and salt. Pour over the pecans in the pie shell, being careful not to disturb their pattern. They will rise to the surface.

4. Bake for 10 minutes, then reduce the oven temperature to 350°. Continue baking for 30 minutes. Cool before serving.

Serves 4–6

Coconut Cream Pie

pie pastry made with $1\frac{1}{2}$ cups flour
1 cup sugar
6 tablespoons flour
3 cups lukewarm milk
3 egg yolks
2 tablespoons butter
1 teaspoon vanilla extract
$\frac{3}{4}$ cup shredded coconut

1. Preheat the oven to $425°$. Roll out the dough and use to line a 9 inch pie pan. Bake unfilled for 20 minutes or until golden brown and set. Remove from the oven and cool slightly.

2. Put the sugar and flour in a saucepan and gradually stir in the milk. Cook, stirring, for 10 minutes or until thickened. Cool slightly.

3. Beat the egg yolks with 3 tablespoons of the milk mixture. Stir this into the remaining mixture in the pan. Return to the heat and cook gently, stirring, until the mixture is very thick. Stir in the butter, vanilla, and all but 2 tablespoons of the coconut.

4. Pour the coconut mixture into the pie shell and sprinkle the reserved coconut on top.

5. Bake for 15 minutes. Cool before serving.

Serves 8

Chocolate Chiffon Pie

1 cup Brazil nuts
2 tablespoons sugar
Filling
2 envelopes unflavored gelatin
½ cup sugar
¼ teaspoon salt
1 cup milk
2 eggs, separated
8 oz (8 squares) semisweet chocolate, broken into pieces
1 teaspoon vanilla extract
1½ cups whipping cream
2 tablespoons chopped Brazil nuts

1. Preheat the oven to 400°. Grind the nuts in a food mill or blender. Mix with the sugar, then press over the bottom and sides of a 9 inch pie pan. Bake the nut crust for 8–10 minutes or until lightly browned. Cool.

2. For the filling, put the gelatin, half the sugar, and the salt in the top of a double boiler. Stir in the milk, egg yolks, and chocolate. Cook, stirring, until the gelatin has dissolved and the chocolate has melted. Remove from the heat and stir in the vanilla. Cool the chocolate mixture, then chill until it is on the point of setting.

3. Whip the cream until thick. Fold about two-thirds of the cream into the chocolate mixture. Beat the egg whites until stiff. Add the remaining sugar and beat for a further 1 minute. Fold the egg whites into the chocolate mixture. Pour the filling into the pie shell. Chill for 3 hours or until set.

4. Decorate with the remaining whipped cream and the chopped Brazil nuts.

Serves 6–8

Angel Cake

$\frac{3}{4}$ *cup flour*
1 tablespoon cornstarch
$\frac{1}{2}$ *teaspoon ground cinnamon*
1 cup sugar
10 egg whites
1 tablespoon lemon juice
1 tablespoon hot water
1 teaspoon cream of tartar
grated rind of 2 oranges
$\frac{1}{2}$ *lb strawberries, hulled*
confectioners' sugar

1. Preheat the oven to 350°. Sift the flour, cornstarch, a little salt, and cinnamon into a mixing bowl. Add about one-third of the sugar. Sift these ingredients twice more.

2. Divide the egg whites, lemon juice, and hot water between two large mixing bowls. Beat the contents of one bowl until foamy, then add half the cream of tartar and continue beating until the mixture will stand in stiff peaks. Beat the contents of the second bowl in the same way, adding the remaining cream of tartar. Tip into the first mixture.

3. Sift in the remaining sugar and the orange rind and beat for 1 minute. Gently fold in the flour mixture. Spoon into an $8\frac{1}{2}$ inch angel cake or tube pan that is 4 inches deep. Bake for 45 minutes or until the cake will spring back when lightly pressed.

4. Remove the cake from the oven and invert it over a bottle or some other tall object. Cool completely.

5. Remove the cake from the pan and place it on a serving plate. Fill the center with the strawberries and sprinkle with confectioners' sugar.

Serves 8

Devil's Food Cake

4 oz (4 squares) semisweet chocolate
1 cup milk
1 cup brown sugar
1 egg yolk
2 eggs, separated
2½ cups flour
¼ teaspoon salt
1 teaspoon baking soda
8 tablespoons (1 stick) butter
¾ cup granulated sugar
¼ cup water
1 teaspoon vanilla extract
1 package fudge frosting

1. Preheat the oven to 350°. Put the chocolate, milk, sugar, and 1 egg yolk in the top of a double boiler. Cook, stirring, until the chocolate melts and thickens slightly. Remove from the heat.

2. Sift the flour, salt, and soda into a mixing bowl. In another bowl, cream the butter with the granulated sugar until the mixture is light and fluffy. Beat in the remaining egg yolks, then add the flour and water and mix to make a smooth batter. Stir in the vanilla and the chocolate mixture.

3. Beat the egg whites until stiff and fold them into the batter. Divide the batter between three greased and floured 8 inch layer cake pans. Bake for 25 minutes or until a skewer inserted into the centers of the cake layers comes out clean. Cool on a cake rack.

4. Make the frosting according to package instructions. Sandwich the cake layers together with about three-quarters of the frosting. Use the remainder to cover the top and sides of the cake, swirling it into a decorative pattern.

Serves 8

BREADS & COOKIES

San Francisco Sourdough Bread

12 cups all-purpose or bread flour
2 tablespoons sugar
1½ tablespoons salt
4 cups water
2 tablespoons oil
Starter
2 cups all-purpose or bread flour
½ cup sugar
2 cups milk

1. First make the starter. Put all the ingredients into a screw-top jar and shake to form a smooth paste. Leave, covered, in a warm place for 1 week.

2. Sift the flour, sugar, and salt into a bowl. Add the starter, water, and oil and mix to make a dough. Tip the dough onto a floured surface and knead for about 5 minutes or until the dough is smooth and elastic. Shape into a ball and place in a greased plastic bag. Leave to rise for 2 hours.

3. Preheat the oven to 375°. Punch down the dough and knead it for a further 10 minutes. Divide it in half and shape each piece into a round, about 6 inches in diameter.

4. Put the rounds on greased baking sheets. Cut a deep cross in the top of each round. Bake for 1–1¼ hours: it should sound hollow like a drum. Cool on a cake rack.

Makes 2 loaves

Parker House Rolls

1 package active dry yeast
6 tablespoons sugar
2 teaspoons lukewarm water
1½ cups milk
9 tablespoons butter
6 cups flour
1 teaspoon salt
1 egg, beaten

1. Mix the yeast with ½ teaspoon of the sugar and the water. Leave in a warm place until the mixture is frothy. Scald the milk in a saucepan. Remove from the heat and add 6 tablespoons of the butter. Stir until the butter has melted, then leave the mixture to cool to lukewarm.

2. Sift the flour, salt, and remaining sugar into a mixing bowl. Add the yeast and milk mixtures and the egg and mix to a dough. Tip the dough onto a floured surface and knead for 10 minutes or until smooth and elastic. Shape the dough into a ball and place it in a greased plastic bag. Leave to rise for 2 hours.

3. Punch down the dough and knead it for a further 3 minutes. Roll it out to about ½ inch thick. Spread 2 tablespoons of the remaining butter over the dough, then cut it into 3 inch rounds. Make a shallow cut in the center of each round and fold into semi-circles, pressing the edges together to seal.

4. Place the rolls on greased baking sheets, spacing them well apart. Melt the remaining butter and brush it over the rolls. Cover and let rise for 45 minutes.

5. Preheat the oven to 475°. Bake the rolls for 15–20 minutes or until golden brown.

Makes about 40

Spoon Bread

1 cup white cornmeal
1 teaspoon baking powder
¼ teaspoon baking soda
½ teaspoon salt
3 eggs, beaten
2 cups buttermilk
2 tablespoons butter

1. Preheat the oven to 400°. Sift the cornmeal, baking powder, soda, and salt into a mixing bowl. Add the eggs and mix well, then gradually beat in the buttermilk to make a smooth batter.

2. Put the butter in an 8 × 8 × 2 inch baking pan or a 1½ quart capacity soufflé dish. Warm in the oven until the butter has melted.

3. Remove the pan or dish from the oven and tilt it to coat the bottom and sides with melted butter. Pour any excess butter into the cornmeal batter and stir it in, then pour the batter into the pan or dish.

4. Bake for 35 minutes and serve hot.

Serves 4

Blueberry Muffins

3½ cups flour
1½ teaspoons salt
¾ cup sugar
4 teaspoons baking powder
4 eggs
8 tablespoons (1 stick) butter, melted
1¼ cups milk
1½ cups blueberries

1. Preheat the oven to 450°. Sift the flour, salt, sugar, and baking powder into a mixing bowl.

2. In another bowl, beat the eggs until they are pale and thick. Beat in the melted butter and milk followed by the flour mixture. Do not overbeat: the ingredients should be just combined.

3. Coat the blueberries lightly in a little extra flour (this prevents them sinking to the bottom of the muffins), then fold them into the batter.

4. Divide the batter between 36 greased and floured muffin pans. Bake for 15 minutes or until risen and golden brown. Serve hot.

Makes 36

Brownies

6 oz (6 squares) semisweet chocolate
2 tablespoons water
8 tablespoons (1 stick) butter
½ cup sugar
1 teaspoon vanilla extract
1 cup self-rising flour
2 eggs
½ cup chopped walnuts

1. Preheat the oven to 325°. Put the chocolate, water, and butter in a saucepan and heat gently, stirring until the mixture is smooth. Remove from the heat and stir in the sugar and vanilla. Cool slightly.

2. Sift the flour and a pinch of salt into a mixing bowl. Add the eggs and chocolate mixture and beat until smooth. Fold in the walnuts.

3. Pour into a greased 8 inch square baking pan. Bake for 30–35 minutes or until a skewer inserted into the center comes out clean.

4. Cool in the pan, then cut into squares to serve.

Makes about 16

(Top) Brownies
(Bottom) Chocolate Chip Cookies

Chocolate Chip Cookies

---

8 tablespoons (1 stick) butter
½ cup granulated sugar
½ cup brown sugar
1 egg
½ teaspoon vanilla extract
1½ cups flour
½ teaspoon salt
½ teaspoon baking soda
½ cup chopped walnuts
½ cup chocolate chips

1. Preheat the oven to 375°. Cream the butter with the sugars until the mixture is light and fluffy. Beat in the egg and vanilla.

2. Sift the flour with the salt and baking soda, then add to the butter mixture. Beat until smooth. Mix in the walnuts and chocolate chips.

3. Drop teaspoons of the mixture onto greased baking sheets, spacing them well apart to allow for spreading. Bake for 10–15 minutes or until the cookies are golden brown. Cool on a cake rack.

Makes about 30

Pretzels

1 package active dry yeast
½ teaspoon sugar
1 cup lukewarm milk
2 tablespoons butter
3 cups flour
½ teaspoon salt
1 tablespoon caraway seeds
1 egg, beaten

1. Mix the yeast with the sugar and 2 tablespoons of the milk. Leave in a warm place until frothy. Scald the remaining milk in a pan. Remove from the heat and add the butter. Stir until the butter has melted, then leave to cool to lukewarm.

3. Sift the flour and salt into a mixing bowl. Add 2 teaspoons of the caraway seeds and the yeast and milk mixtures. Mix to a dough. Tip onto a floured surface and knead for 10 minutes or until smooth and elastic. Shape into a ball and place it in a greased plastic bag. Leave to rise for 45 minutes.

4. Punch down the dough and knead for a further 3 minutes. Roll into a sausage about 1 foot long. Cut the roll into 48 pieces. Roll each piece into a thin sausage about 6 inches long. Put on a flat surface and curve the ends towards you. Cross the loop halfway along each side and twist once. Bend the ends back and press firmly onto the curve of the loop.

5. Preheat the oven to 375°. Drop the pretzels, a few at a time, into a pan of boiling water and cook until they rise to the surface. Remove and drain on paper towels. When all the pretzels have been 'boiled', arrange them on greased baking sheets.

6. Coat with beaten egg and the remaining caraway. Bake for 15 minutes or until golden brown. Cool on cake racks.

Makes 48

INDEX